HALL OF FAITH SERIES

Trailblazer For Jesus

PATRICIA MAXWELL

HALL OF FAITH SERIES

Trailblazer For Jesus

PATRICIA MAXWELL

Pacific Press Publishing Association
Boise, Idaho
Oshawa, Ontario, Canada

Cover art and inside illustrations by Sue Rother
Design by Consuelo Udave

Copyright © 1981
Pacific Press Publishing Association
Litho in United States of America
All Rights Reserved
ISBN 0-8163-0374-6

This book was first published in the
Trailblazer series under the title,
A Soldier for Jesus

87 88 89 90 91 ● 5 4 3 2 1

Library of Congress Cataloging in Publication Data

Maxwell, Patricia, 1935-
  A soldier for Jesus.

  (Trailblazers for Jesus series)
  SUMMARY: A biography of the first Seventh-day Adventist missionary who left America with his son and daughter in 1874 to begin working for Jesus in Switzerland.
  1. Andrews, John Nevins, 1829-1883—Juvenile literature. 2. Seventh-day Adventists—Biography—Juvenile literature. [1. Andrews, John Nevins, 1829-1883. 2. Missionaries. 3. Seventh-day Adventists] I. Title. II. Series.
BX6193.A5M39   266'.673 [B] [92]   80-16753
ISBN 0-8163-0374-6

Contents

Prayer for a Crippled Boy 9
Treatments and Stories 17
Mother Andrews—A Soldier's Helper 24
The Soldier Who Helped Others 31
The First Camp Meeting 39
Sadness Comes to the Andrews Home 44
All Aboard for Switzerland! 50
Learning to Live in Another Country 59
Printing and Preaching in Europe 66
Faithful to the End 71

Charles Andrews often awoke at night crying out with the pain in his leg.

Prayer for a Crippled Boy

Six-year-old Charles tried to sit up in bed. He couldn't move his foot. Pain shot up his leg, and he cried, "My leg! My leg! It hurts! Oh, how it hurts!"

Then Charles heard his mother walking down the hall. The lantern she carried made dancing shadows on the walls as she came into his room. After setting the lantern on a table beside his bed, she bent over him and patted his forehead. "There, there, Mellie. I'm here to help you now," she said.

Charles's family called him "Mellie" because his middle name was Melville. Besides that, he had an uncle and a great-uncle each named Charles; and everybody got mixed up talking about three different Charleses.

Mother pulled back the quilt and began rubbing Charles's right foot and leg. Up and down, up and down, she moved her hand over his sore leg. Then she rubbed his foot. For a long time Charles's foot had been so stiff that he couldn't move it. It stuck out from his leg like the funny stuffed feet on his sister Mary's rag doll.

"Mother, will I ever get well?" he asked as she rubbed his toes.

Mother stopped rubbing and looked at him. "You know, Mellie," she said, "your father and I have both prayed for you many times."

"But I'm still not better. Doesn't God hear us?"

"Yes, Mellie," Mother answered. "God hears us. We must keep on believing in Him." She ran her fingers through his hair and smiled.

"Tomorrow your father will be home from his preaching trip. Right now you need to go back to sleep so you'll feel good when he comes."

She pulled the quilt up over him and patted his head.

"All right, Mother, but will you pray with me before I go to sleep?" Charles asked.

"Yes, of course," Mother said.

Charles closed his eyes and listened while Mother prayed.

"Please, God, make my son's leg well and strong again. And thank You for hearing my prayer. In Jesus' name. Amen." Then Mother bent over him and kissed him. She picked up her lantern and walked toward the door. "Good night, Mellie," she said as she stopped by his door before going back to her own bedroom.

"Good night, Mother. My leg feels better."

Soon Charles fell asleep again. When he awoke, the sun shone so brightly in his room that he knew it must be late in the morning. He rubbed his eyes. He could hear his mother talking to someone in the kitchen.

Charles lay still in his bed and listened. "It's Father!" he exclaimed. He got out of bed as fast as he could. He couldn't run as he wanted to do. But he hopped quickly toward the kitchen. As soon as he got to the kitchen door, he saw his father turn toward him and hold out his arms.

"How's my boy?" Father asked as he hugged Charles tight.

"Pretty good," Charles answered as he grinned at his father.

"Come and sit down beside me, Mellie," Father said. "I have something to tell you and Mother."

Father helped Charles walk to a chair near the table. Then Father pulled a chair right close to him and put his arm around Charles's shoulders.

"Son," he said, "while I was away, I learned that Mrs. White had a message from the Lord about health. I haven't studied it all yet, but I'm going to. I have learned something that I'd like to try."

"What is it, John?" Mother asked.

Fomentations on Mellie's leg," Father said.

"What are fo— fo— What did you call them, Father?" Charles asked.

Father laughed. "That is a big word, isn't it? It's fo-men-ta-shuns," he said slowly. "We take a wool cloth and dip it into hot water, then put the hot cloth on your leg."

"Let's try it, John," Mother said quickly. "The doctors don't know what to do for Mellie's leg; so we may as well try this treatment. And since the idea comes from the Lord's messenger, Ellen White, it's got to be good!"

"When do we start?" Charles asked.

"Not until you and your father have some breakfast," Mother answered. "Let me get something for both of you to eat."

11

After breakfast Charles's father helped him get back in bed. "Now you just lie here quietly while mother and I fix the fomentation. While it's on your leg, we'll visit."

"Oh, good!" Charles answered. His father had to be away from home on preaching trips so much of the time that it would be very special to have a visit with him.

In a few minutes Mother came in, pulled the quilt back, and laid a towel on his leg.

"Are you ready?" Father called from the kitchen.

"Yes," Mother answered, and soon Father walked into the room with a steaming cloth in his hand.

Charles looked at it and asked, "Will it hurt?"

"No," Father answered. "But it will be quite warm. If it's too hot, just tell me, and I'll lift it off your leg a little."

"O-oh, o-oh, it *is* hot; but I guess it's not too hot," Charles said as his father placed the cloth on his leg.

Father pulled a chair close to Charles's bed and sat down. "I knew you'd take this treatment like a man," he said as he smiled at Charles. "You come from a long line of brave people. The Andrews family came to America 'way back in 1638. They had to be brave to make a trip across the ocean and settle in a wild, new land."

"Do you know any stories about any of them?" Charles asked.

"No, I don't know much about them, except for some trouble they had with the Indians."

"Tell me about it!" Charles begged.

"Well, it's kind of sad," Father said. "One man by the name of Ezra Andrews went out to work in his field one day with his four boys. They carried their guns with them. Nobody ever went out without a gun, because the Indians had been unfriendly for a time. Ezra and his boys set their guns against the stone fence while they hoed the corn. When they got to the far end of the field, away from their guns, Indians ran out of the woods and attacked them. Ezra and the boys were too far away from their guns. They were all killed by the Indians."

"That's terrible," Charles said. "But if they were all killed, how come there are still Andrews people like us?"

Charles's father explained, "One boy by the name of Peter stayed in bed that morning because he was sick. The Indians didn't see Peter or his mother; so they lived. Peter grew up, got married, and had a big family of boys. Those boys got married and had boys and girls of their own, and they grew up and had boys and girls. So there are lots of Andrewses."

Charles smiled. "The cloth on my leg is getting cool now," he said.

"Then we'll ask Mother to bring another hot one," Father replied. After Mother placed another hot cloth on his leg, Charles lay still while his father kept talking.

Did you know that about eighty years ago one of the Andrews boys fought in the American Revolution? His name was David, and he and his best friend, John Nevins, went to war together. Years later, David's great-grandson married John's great-granddaughter. Their names are Edward and Sarah. Do you know who that could be?"

Charles thought a minute. Did he have some relatives named Edward and Sarah? Oh, yes! I know! he thought. "It's Grandpa and Grandma Andrews, isn't it?" Charles asked.

"Yes, it is," Charles's father agreed. "And can you see why they named their first son, which is me, John Nevins Andrews?"

"I'm not sure," Charles answered.

"After my great-great-grandfather, John Nevins, who was the best friend of my other great-great-grandfather, David Andrews."

"But you're not a soldier like they were," Charles said.

"No," his father answered, "but I am a soldier for Jesus. And you can be one too."

"But I'm not named after anybody who fought in the war," Charles replied.

"You're named after your mother's brother Charles," his father explained. "And I had an uncle named Charles. Did I ever tell you about the offer my uncle Charles made me when I was seventeen?"

"No, Father. Tell me about it."

"Why don't we save that for your next treatment time. You're looking a little sleepy right now. I think this treatment has made you sleepy."

Charles yawned, and his father laughed. "See? Those warm cloths on your leg made you sleepy."

"I guess so," Charles answered as he snuggled his chin against the quilt. "You won't forget to tell me about your uncle Charles, will you, Father?"

"No, Son. Before you go to sleep, let's pray and ask God to use these treatments to heal your leg."

Charles closed his eyes while his father prayed for him.

"Dear Lord, please put Your healing hand on my son's leg. Make it well and strong and straight again so he can run and play like other boys. And thank You for hearing our prayers. In Jesus' name. Amen."

As Charles fell asleep, he felt warm and cozy and good inside. His leg didn't hurt either.

Mother and Father put hot fomentations on Charles's leg as Mrs. White had instructed them to do.

Treatments and Stories

That evening, Charles's mother and father fixed more fomentations for his leg. After the fomentations they finished with a cold rubdown. While Charles lay in his bed, his father talked with him.

"Tell me about your uncle Charles, now, Father," he asked.

"First of all, let me tell you about when I was a boy," Father said.

"Oh, good!" Charles said, and his father smiled.

"I was just five years old," Father began; "that's a year younger than you, Mellie, when I got very scared."

Charles shivered a bit. "What happened to you?"

"Would you believe I got scared in church one Sunday morning?" Father laughed.

"How could that be?" Charles replied.

"I remember just as plain as if it were yesterday," Father went on. "I was sitting in church with my father and mother and younger brother. The preacher began his sermon by reading a verse in the Bible that says, 'I saw a great white throne, and him that sat on it, from whose face the earth and the heaven fled away; and there was found no place for them.'"

"What's so scary about that?" Charles asked.

"Well, I could just see myself standing before a huge white throne," Charles's father explained; "I imagined God shaking His finger at me and saying 'Sorry, John, you've been a bad boy. There's no place in heaven for you.' "

His father's answer made Charles a little worried, and he asked, "Is that what's going to happen?"

"No, Mellie." Father shook his head. "We will all stand before God; but we don't need to worry, if we've asked Jesus to save us from our sins. But I didn't know Jesus as my Saviour when I was five years old, and all I could think of was all the naughty things I'd done. So that sermon scared me, but it made me want to be right with God. Not long after that, I joined the Methodist Church. And as soon as I learned to read, I started reading the Bible for myself."

Charles thought about all the big words in the Bible, and he asked his father, "How old were you when you started reading the Bible all by yourself?"

"I really don't remember," Father answered. "I know I got up at four in the morning to read my Bible before I went to school. I really loved school too. In fact I loved to study more than I liked the sports and games my friends played."

"You mean you never played?" Charles asked. "You just read books all the time?"

"No, not quite." Father smiled. "I did go sledding and ice skating with my friends in the winter. In the summer we played along the creek or went fishing. I worked hard on the farm too. My younger brother couldn't work much because he was crippled."

Charles thought about his father's brother and asked, "Do you think my leg will get better so I can play with other boys? Or will I be like your brother?"

Father reached out and squeezed Charles's hand and held it tight. "Son, your mother and I both believe that God is hearing our prayers for you and that these treatments are going to help you. Your leg doesn't seem to hurt you as much after you've had some fomentations, does it?"

"It doesn't, Father. At least not for a while," Charles agreed.

Father squeezed his hand again and smiled. "Say, wasn't I going to tell you about my uncle Charles?"

"Oh, yes, tell me about him!"

"My uncle Charles had a lot of money. He was a member of Congress. Congress is the group of men, Mellie, who go to Washington, D.C., to make the laws for our country. My parents were very poor; and even though Uncle Charles and Aunt Hanna lived nearby in the town of Paris, Maine, it was like going into a different world to visit their fancy home. Aunt Hanna had fine lace tablecloths and a maid who cleaned house for her and fixed the meals."

"I wish I had a maid," a voice down the hall said. Charles and his father both turned their heads toward the door just as Charles's mother walked into the room with another hot fomentation in her hands. She laughed. "What are you two talking about? Maids and lace tablecloths and such things!"

"Father's telling me about when he was a boy and about his rich uncle." Charles smiled up at his mother. "Maybe I'll grow up and be rich because I've got the same name."

His mother and father both laughed.

Mother placed the hot cloth on his leg and,

straightening up said, "I'd rather have a kind, loving Christian man like your father than a rich one."

Charles's father put his arm around her, and they both stood close to each other next to Charles's bed. Then his mother moved away, saying, "I've got to put little Mary to bed. I'll leave you men to your talk."

As Charles's mother left the room, she called back, "Since you can't tell him you're rich, John, you ought to at least tell him how brave you are. Like the time you saved that old man from a beating."

"What beating? What man? What did you do?" Charles asked three questions all at once—he was so curious.

"Your mother thinks I'm a hero." Charles's father laughed. "It really wasn't much. No more than any Christian would do."

"But tell me, Father, please!" Charles begged.

"I guess I was about fourteen when it happened," Father began. "I was walking to a meeting with Brother Davis, an old man who belonged to our group of advent believers. My family and I no longer belonged to the Methodist church. We heard William Miller preach that Jesus was coming in 1844. The more we studied our Bibles, the more we believed in the soon coming of Jesus too. But the Methodist Church didn't believe the same as we; so we stopped going to that church. Instead, we met with other people who believed in the soon coming of Jesus. We held meetings in the schoolhouse.

"Anyway, Brother Davis and I were walking together to a meeting in the schoolhouse one evening. Some of the neighbors and people around town made fun of those of us who believed Jesus was coming soon. But this one evening they did more than just call us names.

"Just as Brother Davis and I reached the bridge, a mob of angry men ran out of the bushes and straight at us. They surrounded us so we couldn't go across the bridge or run back the way we had come. We both stood still wondering what would happen next. One of the men rushed at us swinging a large horsewhip. It hit Brother Davis on his legs. I couldn't stand to see those men hurting an old man; so I put my arm around Brother Davis and said, 'We are told in the Bible to bear one another's burdens. If you whip Brother Davis, you whip me too.'

"The man dropped his horsewhip and told us to go on. As we passed, I heard him say, 'It is too bad to whip a boy.'"

"Whew!" Charles said, "That was a brave thing to do, Father."

"I'm sure you'd be brave too, Mellie, for the Lord and His people. As brave as a soldier. But, say, didn't I start to tell you about Uncle Charles?"

"Yes, yes," Charles answered. "Please finish telling me about Uncle Charles."

Father stroked his beard and said, "Let's see, I was telling you Uncle Charles had a lot of money. He was a member of Congress. One day he drove out to our farm to see me. I was out cutting hay in the south pasture. He walked out to the pasture just to see me. 'What do you plan to be in life?' he asked me. I was only seventeen, but I knew exactly what I wanted to be. 'I've decided to be a minister,' I told my uncle.

"Uncle Charles didn't look too pleased when I told him that. 'I've heard that you worship on the seventh day of the week as the Jews do,' he said. 'Surely you don't plan to preach about going to church on Saturday, do you?'

"'Since that's what I believe,' I told him, 'that's what I'll preach.'

"What did your uncle say then?" Charles asked.

"He said, 'Look, John, I've got something a lot bigger and better for you than being a preacher who goes to church on the wrong day.'"

"What did he have for you?" Charles asked.

"Well, Son, he said that he'd pay for everything I needed to go to a big school and become a lawyer. Then I could be a Congress member like him and make a lot of money myself and be famous."

"What did you tell him?" Charles wanted to know.

"I wanted to be polite," Father said; "so I told him I'd think about it. Later on I talked it over with my mother and father, and we told Uncle Charles that I felt God wanted me to be a preacher. I'll never forget what Uncle Charles said when he left."

"What did he say?" Charles was anxious to know.

"He said, 'I know you could be a great lawyer, John, but if you go on preaching for these people who go to church on Saturday, no one will ever hear of you.'"

"That's not so, is it, Father?" Charles said. "Lots and lots of people have heard of you. You go ever so many places preaching and telling people about Jesus."

Father smiled. "Yes, I guess a lot of people have heard me and know about me. But you know, Son, the thing that really makes a man great is if he does what God wants him to do." He leaned over the bed, pulled the quilt back, and lifted the cloth off Charles's leg. "I think this treatment is done now," he said. "Let's get you up, and I'll help you walk to the kitchen."

Charles sat up in bed, slid over to the edge, put his feet on the floor, and stood up. "Look at my foot, Father. I think I can move it a little."

"Why, you can! You can!" Father looked very happy. "Come, let's show Mother!" They walked arm in arm to the kitchen. Father called out before they even got there, "Angeline! Look at Mellie's foot! He can move it a little!"

Mother ran to them and knelt down in front of Charles. "Let me see, Mellie," she said.

Charles looked down at his foot and moved it ever so little up and down. His mother threw her arms around him. "Oh, Son, you *can* move your foot a little! God is answering our prayers! These treatments are working!"

Mother Andrews—
A Soldier's Helper

The next morning Charles's mother came to his room to give him his hot-and-cold treatments.

"Your father has a lot of writing to do today," she said. "The *Review and Herald* editor wants him to write many more stories about his preaching trips and about the Sabbath. So I'll talk to you this morning while we treat your leg."

"I did want to hear more about when Father was a boy," Charles said; "but maybe you can tell me about when you were a little girl."

Mother smiled. "I think I can tell you some more things about your father too. We did live in the same town."

"I didn't know that!" Charles said.

"Yes," his mother answered. "We both grew up in Paris, Maine; and both our families heard and believed William Miller's preaching that Jesus would come in 1844. Your father really studied the Bible; and by the time he was fourteen, he had become quite a leader in our little group of believers in Paris. He could preach very well even then. Many times he talked at our meetings about the soon coming of Jesus. He was so sure Jesus would come that year."

"But Jesus didn't come then, did He?" Charles asked.

"No, He didn't." Mother sighed. "A lot of people felt so sad that they stopped coming to church. But not your father. He felt sad too, but he kept right on studying his Bible. He was one of the first ones to start keeping the Sabbath. Even before James and Ellen White started keeping the Sabbath, your father was keeping it."

"Really?" Charles asked.

"Yes, Son. Your father has always lived by what the Bible says. And when he learned that the Bible says we should keep the seventh-day Sabbath, he started keeping it. Marian, a girl about his age, and her brother, Oswald, read a paper about the Sabbath and started keeping it. Then they showed the paper to your father. He studied it carefully and looked up all the texts in the Bible about the Sabbath. Then he talked to his parents about it, and soon his family as well as Marian's family was keeping the Sabbath. Right away, your father started preaching about it, and soon my family and others believed it too."

"Excuse me, Mother," Charles said, "but my hot cloth is getting kind of cold."

"I'll get another one, then," Mother said as she took the cold one off and went to the kitchen. She soon came back and put another hot one on his leg. "How's that?" she asked.

"Fine," Charles answered. "Please tell me some more about Father now."

Mother laughed. "You don't have to beg me to do that, because I love to talk about your father. He'd never admit it, but he's one of the greatest leaders in our church. And he started so young. Why, by the time he was twenty-one, he was preaching everywhere. He and Joseph Bates took a trip through Maine, New Hampshire, Vermont, and even into Canada. When they finished that trip, he wanted to go to Pennsylvania to preach. He didn't feel well. He had a bad cough and was awfully skinny. Hiram Edson took one look at him and said, 'You must slow down and get more rest.' But do you know what your father said?"

"I can guess," Charles answered, grinning at his mother.

"He said, 'How can I rest when souls are dying who do not know Jesus?' So Hiram and your father started out. I read one of the letters Hiram wrote about that trip. He said the roads were full of stumps and logs and mud holes. In Hiram's buggy they climbed up steep mountains and crossed deep valleys. Sometimes fallen trees reached across from one bank to the other right over their heads. In spite of bad roads and wild country, they traveled about 600 miles. Whenever they came to a town, they'd invite people to a meeting in the evening. John, your father, would preach. At the end of the sermon Hiram would ask if there was anybody they could stay with for the night. Somebody would usually offer them some sort of place to stay. Lots of times they'd roll out their blankets on the hard floor. Sometimes they stayed in unused cabins. Some mornings they'd wake up with frost all over their beards."

"Brrrr," Charles said. "I wouldn't want to sleep where it was that cold."

"Me either," Mother agreed. "But your father did.

And lots of times he'd stay up till late at night or early in the morning, writing for the *Review and Herald* paper. Hiram tried very hard to get him to rest. 'You're wearing yourself out, John,' he'd say. 'Can't you forget the paper for a time?' "

"But Father didn't forget about writing for the paper or about preaching, did he?" Charles asked.

"No, he didn't" his mother answered. "And he did wear himself out. When he came back to his hometown after five years of preaching trips, he looked so bad that I hardly knew him."

"What did he look like?" Charles wanted to know.

"I'll never forget how sick he looked," his mother said. "He came to see me right after he got back to Paris, Maine. When I opened the door, there he stood on the front porch looking like an old man. He walked with a cane, all stooped over. And his eyes were so bad that he couldn't read. He really looked awful for someone only 26 years old."

Charles heard footsteps in the hall. He looked toward the door of his room just as his father walked in.

"I needed a break from writing; so I came to see how my boy is doing today." Father smiled at Charles.

"Are you sure you didn't come in here because I was talking about you?" Mother's laugh sounded like silvery bells.

"No," Father answered. "I didn't hear a word you said, but I hope you didn't tell him all my faults!"

"Oh, no, she didn't tell about any faults," Charles said. "Mother told me how hard you worked going places to preach. She said you worked so hard you looked like an old man when you came to see her."

"I did look and feel pretty bad," Father agreed. "But being around your mother made me feel better fast!"

"Did she doctor you like she does me?" Charles wanted to know.

"Not quite the same," Father said; "but she surely helped me. And she still does." Father patted Mother's hand as he spoke. "Why don't you let me sit and visit with Mellie now? You have lots of other things to do."

"All right, John," Mother said. "I do need to peel some potatoes for dinner."

After Charles's mother left the room, his father said, "Your mother really has helped me more than anyone on earth. I don't know why she took to me when I came to her all broken down in health. But she did. And before long we found that we both loved each other. But about that time my family moved to Waukon, Iowa, while her family stayed in Paris, Maine. I surely hated to leave her."

"Why did you move to Iowa?" Charles asked.

Charles's father pulled a chair close to the bed and sat down. "We read in the *Review and Herald* paper that farmland was really good in Iowa and that Adventists could do a lot of good among the settlers there. The prairie grass was hard to dig up, but the soil underneath was good. The ground was easy to plow. Not full of rocks as it is in Maine. But the winters were cold. The wind blew from the north and piled snow up above the windows. I worked in my uncle's store that winter. In the spring my father and I plowed large fields and planted grain. The outdoor work and the rest from preaching must have been good for me because I began to feel much better. When summer came, your mother's family moved to Waukon; and I really felt better then! In fact, I felt so good that I asked her to marry me. We got married that fall after the crops were in. I planned to take out a claim of land and settle down, but the Lord had other plans for my life."

Father stopped talking and reached over and felt Charles's leg. "I think the hot cloths have been on your leg long enough for this time. We'll have a cold rubdown, and then let's take a walk. The sun is out."

"Oh, good! I'd like that!" Charles said.

Father took the damp cloth off his leg. Charles got out of bed and walked across his room to get his clothes.

"Son, you're walking better," Father said. "You don't seem to be limping so much."

"My leg doesn't hurt either," Charles answered.

After Charles put on his clothes, he and his father walked toward the front door. Charles's little sister, Mary, sat in the living room playing with her rag doll. When she saw Charles and his father, she jumped up and ran to them. "I go too," she said.

Father grabbed her into his arms and said, "Sure. You can come too."

The three of them walked outside. Two-year-old Mary wanted to run in the grass; so her father put her down. She started chasing a butterfly. Charles wished he could run as his sister did. Would his leg never get well? he wondered. Or would he be a cripple all his life like his father's brother?

"Someday," Father Andrews told Charles, "you will be able to walk and run just as Mary does."

The Soldier Who Helped Others

Charles and his father watched Mary run after the butterfly. "I really believe you're going to be able to run like that before long, Mellie," Father spoke up.

"Do you really?" Charles asked.

"Yes, I do," his father answered. "Your leg is getting much better since we started the treatments. You'll be as good as new before you know it. Speaking of new, I remember when you were brand new. I thought you were the cutest baby I'd ever seen."

Charles grinned.

"You were born in Waukon, Iowa, October 5, 1857, right there at Grandpa and Grandma Stevens's house," his father told him. "They loved you almost as much as mother and I did. And it's a good thing they did, because soon I had to make more preaching trips. I'd be gone for a long time, but I knew Grandpa and Grandma Stevens and Grandpa and Grandma Andrews would take good care of you and Mother. I got very lonely for you and Mother. And I know Mother missed me. She wrote letters to me all the time. She always said how much she missed me, but she wanted me to do what God wanted me to do. She'd write and tell me things about you too, Mellie.

Like how you learned to walk and get into things. You loved to play with the pots and pans in the kitchen."

Charles laughed. "That's what Mary does now!"

His father smiled at him. "I guess that's something all children like to do when they're two years old."

Mary had stopped chasing the butterfly and had found a patch of daisies that grew along the fence. When Charles and his father came near her, she held up a handful of daisies and said, "These are for Mamma."

"That's nice, Mary," Father said. "I know Mamma will like them."

"You know what I wish?" Charles asked.

"No, what do you wish?" his father asked.

"I wish we still lived near our Grandpas and Grandmas."

"I do too," Father said. "But we moved here to Rochester, New York, because this town is closer to my work. I can get home more often to see you and Mary and Mother than I could when we lived in Iowa. Besides that, the church people from all over the country sent in money and bought this house for us so we could be together more."

"You mean people just gave us this house?" Charles asked.

"Yes, they did." Father nodded. "I certainly never asked them to do this. In fact, I felt embarrassed at having them do it; but I couldn't refuse their gift of love. Say, I think we'd better start walking back to the house now, Mellie. We don't want to wear out your leg, even if it is feeling and looking better."

Every day after that, Charles took a walk after his treatments were finished. Before long he could walk quite a long time without his leg getting tired. Every day it seemed that his leg got better. Pretty soon his foot didn't stick out sideways like the funny stiff foot on Mary's rag doll. It didn't hurt anymore at night either.

"It's a miracle," Mother and Father both exclaimed.

"If this treatment works so well, we ought to do the other things Ellen White says about health," Charles's father decided. The family stopped eating meat and started eating more fruits and vegetables. Charles's mother learned to bake good whole wheat bread. Soon the whole family felt better. They didn't get sick so often.

And before many months passed, Charles's leg was as good as new, just as his father had said. Charles could run even faster than Mary. By the time he was eight years old, he could run and play like other boys his age.

One hot summer day Charles ran into the kitchen to see if dinner was ready. As he shut the door behind him, he heard his mother ask, "How soon must you leave, John?"

Charles stopped short. "Where are you going this time, Father?" Charles wanted to know.

"This is a very special trip, Son," Father answered. "The church has asked me to go to Washington, D.C. and talk to the leaders of our country."

"Are you going to talk to the President of the United States?" Charles asked.

His father laughed. "I don't think I'll get to talk to the President. But I hope to talk to some of his helpers."

This trip sounded like a very important one; so

Charles asked, "What are you going to talk about?"

His father answered, "The church has asked me to talk about our Seventh-day Adventist boys who are having to go to the Army and fight in the Civil War. You know, Mellie, that the Bible says we are not to kill, yet the Army says that all soldiers must carry a gun and learn to kill. We are going to ask the leaders of our country if they won't excuse our boys from carrying guns and let them do something else."

"What else would they do?" Charles wanted to know.

"They could take care of sick or hurt soldiers," his father said. "I'm sure the Army could find plenty of things for our boys to do. There are other churches, like the Quakers, who do not have to carry guns in the Army. If our country can help other people who believe they shouldn't carry guns, then I think they'll help us."

Father turned to Mother and said, "Did I tell you, Angeline, that the governor of Michigan and other important people have written their names on the paper that I'm taking to Washington?"

"Oh, that's good," Mother answered. "But when do you leave?"

"Tomorrow, on the eight-o'clock train."

"It's so hard to see you going all the time," Mother said; "but I know you must do God's work. The children and I will be praying for you."

The next day Charles got up early so he could walk to the train station with his father. He carried his father's suitcase part of the way. When his father got on the train, Charles wished he could go too. He would like to see the capital of the country and be with his father on an important trip.

A few days later when Charles's father came home, he announced, "The Army is not going to make our boys carry guns."

"I'm sure glad," Charles said, "because I don't want to carry a gun when I grow up and go to the Army."

Father put his arms around Charles and said, "I hope this war is over very soon and you never have to go into the Army. But I hope you'll always be a brave soldier for Jesus."

"I will, Father," Charles answered. "Just like you."

For a moment Father sat quietly beside Charles. Then he said, "You know, Mellie, the reason I have to go away from home so much is because of the war that's going on between Jesus and Satan. Satan is busy fighting God's people. In just a few days I must make a trip to New York to visit some of our churches where Satan has been fighting. The church members have been giving in to Satan. They haven't been strong for the Lord. I must go and talk to them and help them be brave fighters for Jesus again."

"I hope you win," Charles said.

"I can't win," his father said; "but Jesus can win. As long as we all follow Jesus, we can all win!"

After that, whenever his father was gone on preaching trips, Charles prayed that his father would win with Jesus.

And Elder John Andrews did win many battles for Jesus. He went everywhere. Sometimes he rode the train. Other times he rode in a buggy. Everywhere he went, he preached and asked people to give their hearts to Jesus. People could see that Elder Andrews loved them and wanted them to be strong Christians. They loved him and listened to him. They could see that he was a strong Christian soldier for Jesus; so they picked him to be their General Conference president in 1867. Charles was ten years old when his father became president of the General Conference of Seventh-day Adventists. He wanted to know what a president for the church did.

"What does a General Conference president do?" he asked just as soon as his father came home and told the family about it.

His father explained: "The General Conference president for the Seventh-day Adventist church is in charge of all the church work in the whole country."

At that time Seventh-day Adventists didn't have any missionaries in other countries, but they did have quite a few churches in the United States.

"The General Conference president will have to go many places to preach," Father said. "But besides preaching the president must look after the other ministers and make sure they are paid. The president must know about our printing work and make sure only good books and papers are printed. He must be in charge of business meetings too."

"Does this mean you'll be away from home more?" Charles's mother asked.

"I'm not sure, Angeline," Father answered. "I know I'll still have to visit our churches in many places. And I'll hold tent meetings every summer as I always have. But wherever the Lords sends me, I'll always be thinking of you and praying for you." Father put his arm around her. Then he reached out and drew Charles and little Mary close to him. "And I'll always be thinking and praying for you children too. To know that my family loves me and is praying for me is a great help to me in my work."

Charles wondered how that could be much help. He felt sure he could help his father a lot more if he could go with him sometimes on his preaching trips.

Mother, Charles, and Mary were excited when they saw the place where the meetings would be held and the tents where the people would live.

The First Camp Meeting

One time when Elder Andrews came home from a trip he told the family, "We're going to have a camp meeting."

"What's a camp meeting?" Charles asked, looking up in surprise. "What's a camp meeting?" he asked again.

"You just wait and see," his father answered. "But I know you'll like it. You children will need to help your mother and me get ready, because we've got to go quite a ways to the camp meeting."

"How far?" Mary asked.

At the same time Charles asked, "Will we be gone a long time?"

"It's going to be held in a maple grove in Michigan," Father said. "We'll have it the first week of September. Church people from many places will come, and we'll meet outdoors."

"Outdoors!" Charles said. "Do we get to sleep outdoors and eat outdoors?"

Father laughed. "Yes. Almost everything will be outdoors. But we will have tents to sleep in. Each church will bring its own big tent. We'll hang sheets down the middle of the tents to make two rooms. The men can sleep in one big room and the women in another."

"Where will I sleep?" Charles asked.

"If you like, you can sleep with me," his father answered.

"I want to sleep with Mother," Mary said, hugging Mother as she spoke.

Both Charles and Mary could hardly wait to go to camp meeting. Since their father was the General Conference president, he went early to help get everything ready. When Charles and Mary and their mother got to the campground, their father was waiting for them.

"Let me show you around," he said.

The four of them walked through the campground. At the very center of the campground Father showed them an open space with log benches set in rows. "This is where we will have the meetings," he told them. "Up there is where the speakers will sit."

Charles looked in the direction his father pointed. He saw a wooden platform with a cloth roof over it. He saw something that looked very strange to him; so he asked, "What are those boxes on poles all around the edge of the meeting place?"

"Those are for light," his father said. "On top of each pole is a box filled with dirt. We will built fires in the boxes on top of the dirt. The fires will give us light so we'll be able to see."

"Don't you think it might be kind of cool to sit outdoors at night?" Mother asked.

"In case it gets cold," Father answered, "the fires around the edge of the meeting place will keep us warm too."

"Oh, look!" Mary exclaimed. "What are those big tents over there?" She ran toward them, and Charles ran after her. His leg worked so well now that he easily passed her. Of course she was only six and he was ten; so he ought to be able to run faster than she, he thought. He got to one of the big tents and opened the cloth flap at the end and looked inside. The tent was full of hay and straw. "This must be where the horses will stay," he said to Mary as she ran up beside him.

Their father came up behind them and laughed. "No, the horses don't get a tent of their own. But this is hay for them to eat. The straw is not for horses though."

"What's it for?" Charles asked.

"For the campers' beds," his father answered.

"Do we get to sleep on straw?" Mary asked.

"We surely do," Father said. "Come and see." He led them to a part of the campground where there were twenty-two large tents. "These are the church tents," he told them.

"The cloth in them looks very thin," Mother said.

"Elder White told people to bring cloth tents," Father said; "then if we don't have another campmeeting, people can use the cloth to make overalls."

"There's one over there that looks different," Charles said as he pointed.

"Yes, that's a canvas one," his father said. "Our church at Olcott, New York, brought that one."

"Can we go inside one of the tents?" Mary wanted to know.

"Yes," Father said. "Let's go into the one from the church in New York. We'll be staying in it."

Father held up the cloth door at one end of the tent,

and Charles and Mary and their mother walked in. There was a hall right down the center of the tent. The walls of the hall were cloth. Charles pulled open one of the cloth walls and saw straw piled high. "Is this where we sleep?" he asked.

"Yes," Father said. "You and I and the other men from the church will sleep on this side of the tent. We'll make our beds right on this straw. Mother and Mary will sleep right across the hall from us in another bed of straw. And right up here above the hallway is a board where we can put our things."

"This is going to be fun," Charles said.

And it was fun for Charles and Mary and all the other people who came to the very first Seventh-day Adventist camp meeting. One of the things that Charles and Mary liked was the meeting that Elder James White had just for children. He told them stories and helped them learn verses from the Bible. He gave each of them a small book of stories too.

Every night the fires in the boxes on the poles burned brightly, and Charles and Mary and their mother listened to Elder and Mrs. White talk. But the speaker they liked best was their own father, Elder John Andrews, the General Conference president.

Every night after they got into their beds on the straw, Charles and Mary heard their father going to each of the church tents and asking the campers, "Are you all comfortable for the night?"

Charles always fell asleep before his father got through telling everyone good night. But one time he woke up in the middle of the night. The wind blew hard, and it started to rain. Harder and harder it rained, but he didn't get wet. He heard people in other tents getting up and walking around outside. In the morning he found most the campers standing by the fires drying their wet blankets and clothes. The cloth tents hadn't kept the rain out. Everybody in those tents got wet. But Charles and the people in the canvas tent from New York didn't get wet at all. All the other people said, "We'll get canvas tents for the next camp meeting."

Charles and Mary were sorry when the camp meeting ended, but they were glad that everybody wanted to have another camp meeting the next year.

Sadness Comes to the Andrews Home

For two years Elder Andrews was the General Conference president. He traveled more than ever and preached in many places. For months and months he would be gone holding meetings. Charles and Mary and their mother missed him very much.

Then Elder James White became General Conference president, and Elder Andrews could be home more. He still worked very hard. Even when he was home, he was very busy writing papers and books. Long after Charles and Mary had gone to bed, their father would sit at his desk writing and writing. He wanted everyone to know about Jesus. He worked so hard that Elder James White wrote and asked the church people to help Elder Andrews all they could. "He is always trying to do too much," Elder White wrote. So the church people helped Elder Andrews. When he had to go on preaching trips, church people would come and visit Mrs. Andrews and Charles and Mary. They brought fruits and vegetables from their gardens. The men would bring loads of wood so the house would be warm while Elder Andrews was gone. Elder Andrews was happy the church people helped him and his family. He wrote and thanked them for being so kind.

When Charles was fifteen and in high school and Mary still in grade school, Mrs. Andrews became sick. Even though she felt quite miserable at times, she liked to listen to Charles's and Mary's accounts of school happenings and of things they were learning.

More and more of the time Mrs. Andrews was sick. The doctor came many times to see her, but she didn't get better. The doctor would often shake his head when he was about to leave. "I'm sorry. I wish I could do more," he would say.

Elder Andrews began staying home much more so he could be with Mother and help her. Charles and Mary helped too. Mary, though not yet in her teens, cooked all the meals and cleaned house. Charles cut wood and made sure the woodbox was always full of wood to burn in the cookstove.

"What can we do?" the children asked again and again.

"We can pray," Father answered.

And they prayed often that God would give Mother health again.

"The best thing you children can do for your mother is always to be Christians," Father told them. "That would make her very happy."

"I do want always to be a Christian," Charles said.

"And I do too," Mary answered.

It did make Mrs. Andrews happy to know that her children loved Jesus and wanted always to serve Him. They did all they could to make her happy and to help her get well. The doctor did all he could too. But she didn't get well.

And then one morning Mother died.

Charles and Mary and their father were very, very

sad. They didn't think they could ever be happy again. Father wondered how he could take care of Charles and Mary all by himself. The house seemed so lonely without Mrs. Andrews. Soon Charles and Mary and their father moved to another place. The new home was near an academy, where Charles and Mary could both go to school.

Besides going to school, they both worked at home, keeping the house clean, cooking the meals, and trying to make their father happy again. For a long time he felt so sad he couldn't preach or write. But slowly he started to work again. Things began to be more the way they had been, but still there were lonely times for the family. How much they all missed Mother Andrews!

Soon Father got so busy writing a book that he asked Elder Uriah Smith, the editor of the *Review and Herald* paper, to come and help him. Elder Smith and Elder Andrews worked together writing a book about the Sabbath. They worked and worked. When they finished, they had enough material for three books about the Sabbath instead of just one!

Far across the ocean there were people who had heard about Seventh-day Adventists and wanted to know more about what they believed. These people lived on the continent of Europe, in the country of Switzerland. Someone of them had found a copy of the *Review and Herald,* and from it they had learned that there were other Seventh-day Adventists in America. At last one of their number decided to go to America and find out more about the advent message and the seventh-day Sabbath. In the *Review* they had found the name of Elder J. N. Andrews, Battle Creek,

Michigan. His name and address they wrote on a large envelope. With this envelope James Erzberger (Airs-burg-er) went to America. Not being able to speak English, he showed the letter to different ones. At last he arrived in Battle Creek, Michigan, and was taken to the General Conference office, where he met Elder James White.

The Whites, James and Ellen, invited him to stay with them for a while. At first they could not understand each other. But gradually James Erzberger learned English. Then he told the brethren of the people in his country who longed to know more about the message.

Elder Andrews heard James Erzberger tell about the people of Switzerland. He wondered what could be done to help these people. He thought about it a lot. And he told Charles and Mary about it too. "I wonder whom we could send to Switzerland to preach and teach the people there?" he would ask.

"I don't know," Charles would say. "I don't know anybody who can talk their language."

"Whoever goes will have to learn their language after he gets there," Father answered.

"It would be hard to learn a new language," Charles said.

"Yes, but I'm sure it could be done," Father said thoughtfully. "I learned to read Greek and Hebrew when I was just a boy. I used to carry a Greek Bible with me and practice reading it while I plowed."

Charles laughed. "I hope the horses knew where to go!"

"They did!" his father answered. "A person can learn a lot if he makes up his mind to do it."

Weeks and months went by, and still the Seventh-day Adventists in America hadn't decided how to help the people in Switzerland. Some of the church leaders started saying, "Elder Andrews is the man we should send."

But Elder Andrews didn't think he should be the one to go. How could he go when he didn't have a wife to help him anymore? And he wondered where Charles and Mary would go to school in a foreign land.

Then one day Elder Andrews came home and called Charles and Mary. "I've got some important news," he told them. "Come and sit down and let's talk about it."

Charles and Mary sat down at the kitchen table, and their father started talking.

"While I was at the General Conference meeting," he began, "the leaders voted to send me to Switzerland."

"To Switzerland?" Charles and Mary gasped.

"You mean it?" Charles asked.

"Yes, they did," Father said.

"Are you going to go?" Charles asked.

"Yes, I feel that God is speaking to me through our church leaders. But I'm not the only one going. Both of you will go too."

"Both of us?" Charles asked. "Mary is only twelve. But of course I'm sixteen. I can take care of her."

"I'm getting old enough to take care of myself." Mary shrugged her shoulders. "But what will we do over there, Father?"

"I'm not sure yet," Elder Andrews said. "But I know God can use both of you. Your minds are young. I'm sure you will learn the new language sooner than I."

"When do we go?" Charles asked.

"As soon as we can get tickets," Father replied.

When Charles went to bed that night, he could hardly sleep. He kept thinking about going to Switzerland. "At last," he told himself, "I get to go on a trip with Father."

All Aboard for Switzerland

Charles and Mary and their father were very busy getting ready to go to Switzerland. They sold the furniture in their house because they couldn't take it with them on the boat. They packed their clothes and as many books as they could get into their trunk. "I can't go to another country without some books," Charles's father said.

Charles laughed at that. "I don't think you could go anywhere, Father, without a book or two!"

Father smiled back at him. "I think you're right. But I've noticed you and Mary like to read too!" Then after a pause he added, "I wonder when our tickets will arrive. It should be any day now."

One morning when Charles picked up the mail at the post office, he saw a letter from a ship company. "Our tickets are here!" he shouted as he opened the door and burst into the house. His father and Mary both came running toward him. Charles handed the letter to his father, who opened it and read out loud: "Dear Sir: Enclosed are the tickets you requested. You will sail from Boston harbor on the ship *Atlas* on September 15, 1874."

"That's next week!" Mary said.

"Yes, yes, it is," her father answered quietly.

"In just a few days," Charles thought to himself, "I'll be leaving this house, this town, this country. I wonder what it will be like to go so far away." Charles had a strange feeling inside.

His father and sister must have been thinking the same thing, because none of them said anything.

Ministers and church leaders came to see Elder Andrews and talk with him before he left. He would be the first foreign missionary for the Seventh-day Adventist Church, and they all wanted to wish him well. Friends of Charles and Mary came to see them too. Mary cried when she told her friends good-bye. Charles felt sad, too, when he said good-bye to his friends. But he remembered that Father had said that God had a work for all of them to do in Switzerland. They must go if that was where God wanted them.

A crowd of church people went with them to the boat dock. Charles looked around at the workers on the dock carrying boxes and barrels and trunks up the gangplank into the big ship. He watched the ship's crew working on the deck of the ship. He looked at all the people on the dock waiting to get on the ship. "There must be a lot of people going on this ship," he thought to himself. Then he heard his father speak, "Charles, Mary, come here. Elder White wants to pray with us before we leave."

Charles stood close to his father on one side while Mary stood on the other side of him. Elder Andrews put an arm around each of his children. They bowed their heads and listened as Elder White prayed: "Lord, bless these missionaries that we send today." When Elder White finished praying, he patted

It was not easy to say good-bye to all their friends and set sail for a faraway country across the ocean.

Charles on the shoulder and said, "Be true to the Lord, Son." He hugged Mary and said, "Take good care of your father." Then he threw his arms around Elder Andrews and said, "The Lord be with you, brother!"

The ship's whistle blew, and a sailor called out, "All aboard!"

Elder Andrews, Charles, and Mary walked up the gangplank and onto the ship. They stood next to the rail and waved at their friends. The ship's whistle blew again, and Charles saw men on the dock pull in the gangplank. Then they untied the big ship, and it slowly moved away from the dock. The people on the dock waved and waved. Charles watched them while the ship moved farther and farther away until the people on the dock looked like little specks. Soon he couldn't see them at all. He and Mary and their father kept looking and looking until they couldn't see anything but water.

"When will we see our country again, Father?" Charles asked.

"I don't know, Son. It may be years. But we'll be brave soldiers for Christ, won't we?"

Charles looked at his father and nodded his head. He couldn't say anything because of the strange lump he had in his throat. He looked at Mary. She was wiping her eyes with the lace handkerchief her best friend had given her just before they left. "Come on, Mary," Charles said to her. "Let's look around the ship."

She tried to smile at him, but she couldn't seem to talk much either. So the two of them walked around the ship without saying anything for a while. By the time they got back to their cabin, though, they both wanted to talk at once and tell their father all about the ship.

Before many days had passed, they grew tired of being on the ship. They wondered if they would ever get to where they were going. All there was to see was water, water everywhere! Some days there wasn't even a bird to watch.

"How long will this trip be?" Mary asked Charles one day.

"Father says the ocean trip takes twelve days," Charles told her. "Then we'll get off in England and stay for a while. After that, we'll get aboard ship again. But I don't think it will take very long to sail to France.'"

"But when do we get to Switzerland?" Mary wanted to know.

"I'm not sure how long it will take," Charles said. "When we get to France, we take a train to Switzerland."

"I'll sure be glad to get off this boat," Mary said.

"Me too," Charles answered.

On Sabbath morning Charles thought he saw land. He ran to the cabin and said, "Come on, Mary! I see land! We must be nearly there!"

Mary and Charles ran back to the deck. Their father followed them. The three of them stood by the rail and looked across the water. They could see what looked like a thin, dark line far across the waves. "That's it, children," their father said; "that's England."

Charles and Mary stood on the deck all afternoon watching the line grow bigger. Finally it looked like real hills and trees. By evening the ship had sailed into the harbor and pulled up to a dock. Charles watched the men on the dock tie the ship up, but they didn't put up a gangplank.

"They won't unload us until Monday," Father said when Charles told him about it. "They don't work on Sunday. That's their rest day. Too bad they don't know which is really the Sabbath."

As soon as they left the ship on Monday, they got on a train to London. A man met them there. He had learned to keep the Sabbath when he visited America one time. He took Elder Andrews and Charles and Mary on a trip so that Elder Andrews could preach to the people in his country who wanted to know about Jesus. After a few days Charles and Mary and their father returned to the boat dock and took another ship to France. When they got to France, they got on another train.

"This is the last part of the trip," Charles told Mary.

"Are you sure?" she asked.

"Yes. Father said so."

It was nearly noon when the train reached their new home in Switzerland. Charles looked at the name of the town written above the train station. It said "Neuchâtel."

"How do you say the name of this town?" he asked.

His father said, "I believe you say it like this: Noo-shah-TEL."

"Noo-shah-TEL," Charles said slowly. "It sure is spelled funny."

"We'll see and hear lots of things that we think are funny," Father said; "but we will soon learn how people here talk and think."

"I don't know," Charles said. "I hear everybody talking all around me, and I can't understand one word, not one. I wonder if I'll ever learn the language and understand what these people are saying."

Mary sighed. "Yes, I wonder if we'll ever be able to understand the people."

It didn't take Charles and Mary and their father long to find out they could understand smiles with no trouble at all. For suddenly they saw several people coming toward them with big smiles.

"These must be the people who have been waiting so long for Christian workers from America," Father said.

And he was right. They were the Vuilleumier (Vee-yoo-mee-yea) family. And they took Elder Andrews and his children to their home, where they had a lunch ready for them. They had an apartment in their house, too, where Charles and Mary and their father could live.

That evening Charles stood on the balcony of the apartment and looked out over the city. Not far away he could see a lake.

"That's Lake Neuchâtel," one of the family finally got him to understand. Charles looked at the water sparkling in the sunset. But what he really looked at were the mountains. They seemed to rise right up out of the far side of the lake. Up, up they reached into the sky. Charles had never seen such tall mountains.

"Those are the Alps," his new friends again explained.

Charles looked and looked at the tall mountains. "I wonder how far I could see if I were standing on top of those mountains," he thought to himself. He thought he would like to climb one of the mountains someday and find out.

But there was lots of work to do in Switzerland. And the first job was to learn to talk French. That seemed harder to Charles than climbing a hundred mountains.

Elder Andrews, Charles, and Mary learned to speak French well. Then they studied German.

Learning to Live in Another Country

Charles and Mary and their father had a family council not long after they got to Switzerland. They decided Mary would do the cooking and Charles would go shopping. It seemed like a good plan until Charles got to the marketplace.

He saw rows and rows of vegetables and fruits. But he didn't see any bread or milk. There were cages with chickens in them. And tables piled high with meat and fish. He tried to ask a farmer where to get bread and milk, but the man just looked at him and started talking in French. Charles couldn't understand him; so he went to another farmer. This man just shook his head, shrugged, spread his hands, and said, *"Je ne parle pas l'anglais."*

"Guess he means he doesn't speak English," Charles said. "Now, what to do?" He walked and walked hoping to find someone who could understand him. But he simply couldn't find anybody. They all talked French. Charles knew he must get some food; so he started pointing to things and holding up his money. After a long time he got some potatoes and apples and a small cabbage.

When he got home, Mary asked, "How can I make

Charles could not buy bread or milk at the store. Instead the milkman came with his cow to the door, and the baker brought his bread on a tray every morning.

anything out of that? Didn't you bring any bread or milk?"

"I didn't see any bread or milk," Charles answered. "The people talked so fast in French that I couldn't find out where to get any."

"Maybe the Vuilleumiers can tell us where to get bread and milk," Mary said.

Charles walked downstairs and knocked on the Vuilleumier's door. They smiled and asked him in. They could speak a little English; so he finally got them to understand that he wanted to know where to get bread and milk.

"Oh," they said, "the milkman brings his cow here to our door. You bring a jar out to the front porch every morning, and he will milk the cow and give you how much you need."

"But how do I get bread?"

"From the town bakers," the Vuilleumiers told him. "They come every morning, and you buy it from them."

"It sounds like I'd better be out here in front of the house early every morning," Charles said.

The next morning he stood on the front porch with a jar in his hand. Sure enough, a man came down the street leading a cow. He stopped by the Vuilleumier's door, and Charles held out his jar. The man held it under the cow and began milking. Warm, white milk squirted into the jar until it was full to the top. The man handed the jar full of milk to Charles, and Charles gave him some money. Then the man led his cow to the next house. Charles laughed. "I wonder how many houses the milkman can go to before the cow runs out of milk."

Before long, another man came down the street. He carried a large tray with a white cloth over it. "This must be the bread man," Charles thought; so he waved at the man.

The man saw Charles wave; so he came over to him and lifted the white cloth off the tray. The tray had long loaves of bread on it.

Charles looked for some whole wheat bread because he knew that would be better for them to eat than white bread. But he didn't see any whole wheat bread.

Charles asked, "Do you have any other bread?"

But the man just looked at him and shook his head and said *"Je ne comprend pas l'anglais."*

"I guess he doesn't understand me," Charles thought. "If we're to have any bread, I suppose I'll have to buy some of this."

Charles held out some money and pointed to one of the long, white loaves. The man took the money and handed Charles the loaf of bread.

Charles asked the Vuilleumier family about the bread. They told him that nobody baked his own bread because people didn't have ovens in their houses. "Do any of the bakers make any whole wheat bread?" Charles asked.

"No," they said; "everybody in our country likes this bread."

Because they didn't have much money, Charles and Mary and their father couldn't buy as much food as they needed. In the winter Switzerland gets very, very cold. The family got many colds and sore throats because they didn't have enough good food to eat and because the house was so cold.

Sometimes Charles thought about his home in America and the nice bread his mother used to make. "But I must be a brave soldier for Christ and help Father all I can," he thought.

Charles didn't know how he could help much, when he couldn't speak the language the people of Switzerland spoke. He decided to talk to his father about it.

"We've been here several weeks now," he told his father. "But Mary and I still can't understand what these people are saying."

"You and Mary must learn French as quickly as you can," Father said.

"But how?" Charles asked. "Are you going to send us to a French school?"

"No," his father said. "I'll help you as much as I can, and we'll get Elder Vuilleumier to help us. But the quickest way for all of us to learn French is to stop speaking English."

"How can we do that?" Mary asked. "That's the only language I know. If we don't talk English anymore, I won't be able to say anything."

"It won't be easy, Mary," Father said. "But here's how we'll do it. We will give ourselves only one hour a day, between five and six in the evening, when we can speak English. The rest of the time we must all speak French. To make sure we do it, let's write down our plan and sign our names to it."

"All right," Charles said; "I'll sign my name to it."

"I will too," Mary said. Then she asked "When do we start?"

"We may as well begin first thing tomorrow morning," Father said.

The next day Charles and Mary tried to talk to each other and to their father in French. They carried a French dictionary with them and looked up words so they could say what they wanted to say. But it was hard to find the right French words. And it was hard to remember the French words. Sometimes they got so mixed up in their talking that they just laughed.

All day Charles and Mary looked at the clock, wishing it would go faster so they could talk English. Finally five o'clock came, and they all started talking at one time. They had so much to say. Even their father seemed glad to talk in English. Before they knew it, the hour was gone and their father said, "It's time to go back to French."

"Oh-h-h," groaned Charles. "Will I make it until tomorrow evening?"

His father laughed. "I'm sure you will."

Every day Charles and Mary talked French all day until five o'clock. Soon it started getting easier to talk in French. And before long Charles could understand the people in the marketplace. And soon Mary could talk with the French girls living near them. In fact, Mary got so good at talking French that she sounded just like a French girl.

Elder Andrews learned French well enough so that he could preach in French. And he started going on preaching trips around the country. Everywhere he went, the people were happy to meet him. They listened carefully to the missionary from America.

Seventy-five people were baptized the first year Elder Andrews and Charles and Mary were in Switzerland. This made them glad they had come to Switzerland.

On his eighteenth birthday Charles said to his father and to Mary, "I can't believe we've lived here for more than a year already! And I can talk like these people! And sometimes I feel more like a Swiss person than an American!"

Father and Mary both laughed.

"I guess we're really getting to be missionaries," Mary said.

Printing and Preaching in Europe

One evening Elder Andrews came home with some good news. "I just found out today that there are some people in Germany who are keeping the Sabbath," he said as soon as he walked in the door.

"Really?" Charles asked.

"How did they learn about the Sabbath?" Mary wanted to know.

"We don't know how they learned about the Sabbath," Father answered. "Brother Erzberger and I want to go and see these people right away. He's the one who heard about them. And you'll never guess how he found out about them."

"Did one of them write him a letter?" Charles asked.

"No," his father said, "Brother Erzberger (Airsburg-er) heard about them from a beggar."

"A beggar!" both Charles and Mary said together.

"Yes," their father answered, "a beggar. It seems a beggar came to Brother Erzberger's home. He was looking for a place to stay for the night. Brother Erzberger asked him to come in and started talking with him. He told the beggar about the Sabbath. When the beggar heard about the Sabbath, he got very excited. He said there were some people in his hometown in Germany who kept the Sabbath. Then Brother Erzberger got excited! Anyway, he and I want to go there as soon as we can."

"That's really something," Charles said. "I wonder how many people there are in Germany who are keeping the Sabbath."

Charles didn't get an answer to his question for five weeks. That's how long his father and Brother Erzberger stayed in Germany. When Elder Andrews finally came home, he told Charles and Mary there were forty-six people in the beggar's town in Germany who were keeping the Sabbath.

"And they thought they were the only people in the world who were keeping the Sabbath!" Elder Andrews said. "Brother Erzberger stayed with them so he could teach them more. He knows the German language; so he can help them more than I." Elder Andrews stopped talking for a minute. He seemed to be thinking of something. "You know," he finally said, "we must learn to speak German too."

So Charles and Mary and their father learned to speak German as well as French. And they learned to write in both French and German. Elder Andrews started printing a paper in the French language, and Mary helped him. She was only fourteen, but she had learned French so well that she could help her father with the paper. Elder Andrews wrote most of the stories for the paper, but sometimes some of the other ministers wrote too. Mary read every story for the paper. She looked to see if the words were spelled right. She checked every word to see if it was the right French word to use. Sometimes Mary saw mistakes in the paper. She would make them right. Her father hardly ever made mistakes in his writing, but sometimes some of the other ministers did. They were surprised to find out that Mary and her father knew the French language better than they did.

Charles took the paper to the print shop to get it printed, 2000 copies. He helped fold the papers too, and get them ready to mail.

Many people liked the new paper. They wrote letters and asked for more. Every day Charles walked to the post office and brought home a lot of letters addressed to the editor of the paper. He put them on his father's desk. His father had to stay up late at night to answer all the letters and write more stories for the paper.

One morning when Charles got the mail, he saw a letter from Naples, Italy, a country a long way from Switzerland. He wondered who could be writing from Italy; so he waited for his father to open the letter.

"Praise the Lord!" his father said when he finished reading the letter from Italy. "A doctor way down in Italy got a copy of our paper. He and his family and one other lady have started keeping the Sabbath. They want me to come and baptize them!"

"That's great!" Charles said. "When will you go?"

"I'd like to go soon, but I don't have the money," his father said. "I think I'll write to Elder James White in America and see if the churches in America could send some money so I could take this trip."

Charles knew his father did not like to ask for money. He always tried to save money instead of spend it. Lots of times he didn't eat because he wanted to save money. With the money he saved, he would print more papers.

But he didn't know how he could save enough money to take a long trip to Italy. So he wrote to Elder White in America.

When Elder White got the letter from Elder Andrews, he asked all the church people in America to give. Some time later Elder Andrews received $10,000 to help him print papers and preach to the people in Switzerland and Germany and other places.

It took several months for the money to get to Elder Andrews; so he had to wait to take the trip to Italy. Before the money came, he got sick. Mary and Charles took care of him the best they could, but he didn't get better. At last they called a doctor.

When the doctor saw Elder Andrews, he said "This man hasn't been getting enough to eat! We've got to see that he eats more."

It took some time for Elder Andrews to get well.

Fortunately, when the money from America finally came, Elder Andrews was able to take a trip to Italy. In Italy he baptized the doctor and his family. Then the doctor asked Elder Andrews to print a paper in the Italian language. But Brother Erzberger in Germany wanted Elder Andrews to print a paper in the German language.

How could he find the time to print three papers in three languages every month!

Back in America, Elder James White got to thinking that Elder Andrews should have more help. Soon Elder White and the other ministers in America sent Mr. and Mrs. Ings and Miss Sisley to help Elder Andrews and his family.

Mr. Ings was a printer; so he would be a big help in printing the papers every month. Right away Charles started to help Mr. Ings in the printshop. Charles learned how to run the printing machines and to make the papers look nice.

Mrs. Ings liked to cook; so she fixed the meals and took care of the house. And Mary helped her father more and more with writing the articles for the papers. Everybody kept busy and happy. They were glad that they could be missionaries. Elder Andrews was especially glad to have so much help. He didn't know that he would soon lose one of his best helpers.

Faithful to the End

It seemed that Mary had one cold after another during the winter of 1878. Many days she couldn't help her father write the paper because she had to stay in bed. Elder Andrews felt sure that when summer came, Mary would get better. "She needs more sunshine," he said.

"I think you're right," Charles answered. "As soon as it gets warm enough, I'll take her to the park."

"That's a good idea," Father answered.

"And when summer came, Charles hurried home each day from his work in the printshop so he and Mary could go to the park. But the sunshine didn't seem to help Mary very much. She still coughed and coughed. She felt very tired too. But she wanted to help her father write the paper. She begged him to bring some work home so that she could work while she rested in bed.

Elder Andrews needed Mary's help so very much. Every day Father and Charles prayed that Mary would get well.

"Here's an answer to our prayers," Elder Andrews said one morning when he read his mail.

"What is it?" Charles asked.

Father Andrews and Mary, who was sick, left Switzerland to go home America for a visit. Mary never returned.

"The church leaders in America want me to come to the General Conference meeting in Michigan and tell them about our work here," he said. "If I could take Mary with me, I could have Dr. Kellogg look at her. Surely he could get her well. I couldn't ask the church leaders to pay Mary's way on the boat though. I'll have to pay that."

"I'll help," Charles said. "I've saved a little money."

For the next few weeks Elder Andrews was busier than ever. He worked late every night writing for the paper. He wanted to have enough stories so Charles and Mr. Ings could print the paper for at least two months while he and Mary were in America.

Finally Elder Andrews stopped writing. He hurried home and packed a suitcase for him and Mary.

Charles walked to the train station with them. How he wished he could go to America too, but he was glad his sister could go so she could get well. He stood on the station platform and watched the train slowly start and pull away from the station. Elder Andrews and Mary waved from the window. Charles waved back. He waved and waved until he couldn't see them anymore. "Dear Lord," he prayed as he stood there, "take care of Father and Mary. Please help Mary get well while she's in America. And bring them back real soon."

Charles walked back home. The house seemed very quiet and still. Even though he was twenty years old now, he felt very lonely. But there was a lot of printing work to be done; so he hurried to the printshop and got busy. He knew he had to keep printing and mailing the papers while his father and Mary were gone. They were counting on him to carry on the work. He knew God was counting on him too.

As soon as Elder Andrews got to America, he went to the General Conference meeting. He told the people about the work in Switzerland. He said there were many persons who had learned the Advent Message.

"It's wonderful what you are doing!" the people told him. "We're glad we sent you and your family as our first foreign missionaries."

As soon as the meeting had ended, Elder Andrews took Mary to see Dr. Kellogg. Dr. Kellogg examined Mary a long time. When he finished, he asked the nurses to put her to bed in the hospital. Then he talked to Elder Andrews.

"Elder Andrews," he said "I'm afraid I do not have good news. Your daughter has a bad case of tuberculosis. There is nothing we can do for her. Only God can help her."

Elder Andrews could hardly believe Dr. Kellogg. He stayed right beside Mary's bed every day. The nurses and doctor told him that tuberculosis was a very contagious disease. He should not stay so close to Mary, because he might catch the same sickness.

But Elder Andrews loved Mary and wouldn't leave her.

One evening Mary died. Elder Andrews felt that he could never be happy again. Mary had helped him so much in his work, especially in writing and editing the papers. He didn't see how he could do any more missionary work without her. For weeks and weeks Elder Andrews sat in his home. He didn't feel like preaching or writing or talking to anybody. The church leaders came and tried to make him happy, but he couldn't forget Mary.

Elder Andrews had to write to Charles, who was still in Europe, and tell him that his sister had died. How sad Charles would be when he read that letter, Elder Andrews thought to himself. Charles and Mary had always been such good friends even though they were brother and sister.

All winter Elder Andrews stayed in America. In the spring of the year, almost a year after he had left Europe, he went back to Switzerland. But on the boat he got sick and had to get off in England, where he went to stay with some friends. They took care of him until he got well enough to finish his trip home.

When the train chugged into the station in the town where he lived, Elder Andrews saw his son Charles waiting for him. They threw their arms around each other when they met, and cried. Some of the tears were happy ones because they were together again. But some of the tears were sad because Mary wasn't with them.

Soon after he got home, Elder Andrews got sick again; but he kept working. While he sat in bed, he wrote letters and stories for the paper. It seemed that no matter how sick Elder Andrews got, his mind still worked very well. He knew seven different languages and wrote papers in English, French, German, and Italian. He knew all the New Testament by memory and much of the Old Testament too.

But it seemed as if he would never get to feeling well again. All his life he had worked too hard, but now he tried to take it easy. He often stopped writing and took long walks in the country. Sometimes

Charles walked with him. Charles and his father talked about their missionary work as they walked.

"Your work in the printshop is just as important as my work," Elder Andrews would say. "Printed papers can go many more places than preachers can go. They can go into many, many homes. People can read and become Christians even though we can't send them a preacher."

"How happy I am that I have a part in the mission work here in Europe," Charles often said; "but I do wish you felt better, Father."

Finally, Elder Andrews went to see a doctor in Switzerland. The doctor told him he had the same sickness that Mary had had.

"You probably got it from staying so close to her," the doctor told him. "Did you not know the disease is very contagious?"

But Elder Andrews wasn't sorry he had stayed right beside Mary.

When the church people in America and Europe heard that Elder Andrews had tuberculosis, they had a special day of prayer for him. He got better for a while. But soon he got worse again. Every month it seemed that a miracle happened. When it was time for the paper to be printed, Elder Andrews would be strong enough to write. As soon as he had finished writing the paper, he felt sick and weak again. But he thanked God that he had the strength to write the paper each month.

In the summer the church leaders in America sent more helpers to be with Elder Andrews. His mother, Charles's grandmother Andrews, came to be with them and help them.

One day after lunch Elder Andrews asked for some paper and a pen. But he felt so tired and sick that he could hardly hold the pen. He tried and tried to write. At last he finished and gave the paper to Charles.

When Charles read what his father had written, he smiled even though he felt sad knowing his father was so weak. "This is just like you, Father," he said.

His father had written that when he died he wanted all his money to go to the mission work.

"That's the way you've always been," Charles thought, "always doing all you can for God's work."

That very evening Elder Andrews died.

Now Charles was left all alone. It made him think of Peter Andrews, the boy whose brothers and father had been killed by Indians so long ago.

Charles decided to be brave like Peter and a Christian soldier like his father. He stayed in Switzerland and kept right on working in the printshop. In a few years he married a Swiss girl. Later on they had a baby boy.

When Charles looked down at his tiny son, he said, "I don't ever want to forget what a great soldier for Christ my father was. "Let's name our baby after him. Then there'll be another J. N. Andrews to be a worker for God."

And Charles's little boy did grow up to be a worker for God. He became a missionary doctor. He was a soldier for Christ like his grandfather, John Nevins Andrews, the first Seventh-day Adventist missionary, a true trailblazer.